STRANGE GIRLS

Joanie DiMartino

Poems by

Joanie DiMartino

*For Mr. Elden—
thanks for all you
do for Santo!
All the "strange"
+ the best!
Joanie*

FIRST EDITION

Little Red Tree Publishing, LLC,
635 Ocean Avenue, New London, CT 06320

First Edition, 2010, manufactured in USA
1 2 3 4 5 6 7 8 9 10

Cover and Book Design:
Michael John Linnard, MCSD

All interior photographs are in the public domain and attributed accordingly within the caption of the photograph. Front cover and title page photograph is of *Lulu Lataska, Snake Enchantress*, by Charles Eisenmann, in the public domain. The photograph of the author, which appears on page 122 and the back cover, is by kind permission of Deborah Curtis.

Previous publication:

1. "Great-Aunt Josephine: Lost Photographs" *Calyx: A Journal of Art and Literature by Women* Vol. 21, No. 2, Summer 2003.
2. "carousel in winter" on display at *Collaborations + Catalysts,* an art exhibit displaying collaborative projects with artist Jill Plaistead, Loudon House, Lexington, KY, May, 2005.
3. "carousel in winter" on display, "Divine Woman," originally titled "Sideshow," appeared in exhibit catalogue of the *Sideshow,* an art and poetry exhibit with Mosaic and the Women Artists Group, Carnegie Center for Literacy and Learning, Lexington, KY, March-April, 2005.

Library of Congress Cataloging-in-Publication Data

DiMartino, Joanie.
  Strange girls : poems / by Joanie DiMartino. -- 1st ed.
    p. cm.
  Includes bibliographical references, glossary and index.
  ISBN 978-1-935656-03-6 (pbk. : alk. paper)
  I. Title.
  P3604.I46556S72 2010
  811'.6--dc22

                        2010022282

Little Red Tree Publishing, LLC
635 Ocean Avenue,
New London, CT 06320
website: www.littleredtree.com

DEDICATION

for

Alison McKenna Luff
Valerie Loveland
Sherry Chandler
Rhonda Ward

(sister strange girls)

and

Josephina DiMartino Capone
in memoriam

and

Virginia Pearson
the original
Lady Vishuss

CONTENTS

Foreword by Michael Linnard   viii
Introduction by Joanie DiMartino   x

Invocation   xvi

Leg One - *placing the skull in her hand*

Mermaid   2
Spidora Views Cave Art   4
carousel in winter   5
Lucia Zora Atop Snyder the Elephant   6
Portrait of a Young Woman as Poet   7
Spidora Undergoes *Metamorphosis*   8
Great-Aunt Josephine: Lost Photographs   9
Isabelle Butler Rides *The Dip of Death*   10
The Tattooed Woman   11
Spidora Polishes her Toes   12
When a Circus Troupe Kidnapped María Izquierdo   13
Spidora Embroiders Her Words   14
Aprile and Mae   15
Great-Aunt Josephine: Two-Way Mirror   16

Leg Two - *out of myth, the brazen one*

Mirth & Mayhem   18
Mabel Stark Misses Her Tigers   20
Spidora Finds Religion   21
    Philosophy the First   21
    Arachane, Mother of Spiders   22
    Philosophy of Second   23
    The Solemnity   24
    Philosophy the Third   26
    Praise Song for Anasi's Wife   27
    Philosophy the Fourth   28
    Spider Woman's Gift   29
Lament for Little Miss 1565   30
Clown Psalm   32
Evetta Matthews Clowns Around   33
Eve Eating a Candy Apple   34

Leg Three - *such vile medicine to ingest*

Sword Swallower   36
The Fat Lady Hums to Herself in Autumn   37
Katie Sandwina "Tosses Husband About Like a Biscuit"   38
Popcorn Butcher   39
Spidora Identifies with Flies   41
Great-Aunt Josephine: Savory Gossip   42
Spidora Studies Spiderology   43
An Appetite for Glass   45
Spidora Orders Curds and Whey   46

Leg Four - *like joy corrodes the veins*

Spidora Dances the *Tarantella*   48
Swarm   49
Spidora Rides the *Spider*   50
organ grinder   51
Great-Aunt Josephine: Loose Ends   52
Spidora Sings to Spiders   53
Bird Millman Does *The Charleston*   54
Zazel Blasted Out of a Cannon   55
'Tiny' Kline as Tinker Bell   56

Leg Five - *the gross unfortunate of dusk*

The Gilly Girls in Need   58
Spidora Pulls the Legs Off Spiders   59
mother named Corbin seems very fond of it   61
Divine Woman   63
Spidora Contemplates Children   64
Mrs. Sibilant's Splendid Hair Tonic   65
Spidora Shuns Arachnophobia   66
Little Accuracy   67
Spidora Craves Attention   68

Leg Six - *cropped locks and that curse*

Spidora Visits Mississippi   70
inside the funhouse   72
Spidora Saves Spiders   73
why the two-headed juggler is female   74
Highwire Haiku   75

sleight-of-hand   79
Two Bearded Ladies   80
Josie DeMott Robinson Attends a Rally   82

Leg Seven - *fits of wakefulness when her lust is slaked*

Spidora Covets Silk Stockings   84
After Colette Performs *The Flesh* Outside of Paris   85
Burning Ballerina!   86
Spidora Purchases Pumps   87
Great-Aunt Josephine: Anguine Hours   88
A Treatise on Handling Snakes   89
Spidora Receives a String of Pearls   90
Making Jenny Haniver   91
Lulu Lataska on the Cover   92

Leg Eight - *each night behind closed blinds*

Spidora Defies Description   94
Greasepaint Graces   96
    I   Matilda   96
    II   Petunia   97
    III Allegra   99
Great-Aunt Josephine: First Lesson   101
'Marvelous May' Wirth Somersaults Forward   102
Why Mata Hari Leaves the Circus   103
Contortionist   104
Divorcing the Strong Man   105
As Lillian Leitzel Reaches 249   106
Spidora Embraces Widowhood   107

Epilogue   109

Bibliography   110
Notes on Individual Poems   111
Index of Titles and First Lines   120
About the Poet   124

ACKNOWLEDGEMENTS

I would like to thank Little Red Tree Publishing, Michael Linnard and Tamara Martin, for support, encouragement, friendship, and also for knowing when and how to challenge my creative potential.

Special thanks to:

Mosaic: Sherry Chandler, Tina Parker, Pamela Papka Sexton, Shelda Hale, Margaret Ricketts, Jean-Marie Welch, Karen Koegler, Andrea O'Brien, Susan McDonald, Valerie Loveland, Ann Lederer, and Leah Maines. Women Artists Group (WAG), especially Jill Plaisted, for the collaboration that began this collection. The Poets and Writers Consortium East: Elaine Bentley-Baughn, Jude Rittenhouse, Melanie Greenhouse, Karen Ethier-Waring, Platt Arnold, Susan Zimmerman, and Herta Payson.

My gratitude also to Mike Thomas and Mark Funk; Christie Max Williams and the Arts Café ~ Mystic; James Coleman and Mary Gordon for superb editorial assistance with this manuscript; and Rhonda Ward, for being a Blessing, friend, and poetry champion. To Antoinette Libro, Sue Ellen Thompson, and the late James Baker Hall, I am indebted, always.

I remove my top hat, and give a deep ringmaster's bow to Gregory DeWitt Hardison, professional clown, magician, actor, and friend, for serving as content editor of this project: answering obscure circus questions, recommending books, telling me where my descriptions could be enhanced or corrected, and especially for championing these women, when I felt overwhelmed or struggled with poems.

My deepest thanks are reserved for Michael Hart, for the unconditional love and support of both me and my poetry, and for providing me with a 'room of one's own' when it most mattered; and my son Dante, for being, quite simply, my greatest poem.

FOREWORD

It is a great honor for Little Red Tree to publish this wonderful book of poetry, *Strange Girls*, by Joanie DiMartino.

From the moment I heard Joanie explain to me the ideas and concepts underpinning the book, amidst the post-poetry reading conversational buzz at a crowded Hygienic Galley in New London, on a balmy September evening in 2008, I was caught and "in" for whatever it took to achieve. I loved the idea of the book and its historical focus on a particular group of women who have been, to a large extent ignored, marginalized or discarded from the history books. And then later when I read the first of many drafts and saw the first sepia photograph of Lulu Lataska (front cover), I was determined to produce a book that would do justice to the concept, poetry, poet and the history of these courageous and heroic women.

Now that the book is finished it would remiss of me if I did not express my great pleasure in working with Joanie, and acknowledge her as a truly creative force. Joanie has demanded of herself nothing less than total commitment to achieving the best book possible, without compromising any facet, from the poetic craft and integrity of the space between the words, to the countless hours of research to ensure the historical accuracy of the notes, from the accurate positioning of her poetry on the continuum of philosophical discourse of feminist literature, to the careful consideration of every poems position in relation to every other. Some would consider this excessive or simply "too much," but it is the hallmark of a writer who considers everything and leaves nothing to chance. Joanie comes to poetry with substantial academic credentials as a historian, which was self-evident in the ferocious tenacity she displayed in researching every facet of the lives of the women that she included in the poems but also in the attention to minute detail of the prosody from both an aesthetic, audible and historical sense. As a professional designer I immediately recognized that Joanie was a person who would not accept anything outside or inside the book that appeared by accident. To that extent her involvement in the creation and development process of this book has been total.

It is a book of poetry, with a unique voice, that speaks

directly about and for the spirit of women who fought against, and transcended, the oppression and limitations placed upon them, both physically and psychologically, both societal and personal, and both professional and private, to live a life that expressed their true individuality. It is specifically a book about women and their right to own their bodies and use them in ways that allows them freedom of expression and individual independence.

The fact that Joanie has chosen to present a substantial volume of poetry, which is both eminently accessible, honed, concise and multifaceted in its concept, reaching far into the real politics of feminist literature, is testament to her devotion to the cause of women's rights. This is a wonderful book of poetry written by a woman, about women, for everyone. It reaches back to define a glorious and specific moment in history, and in so doing inform the present, with the hope that it will also propel a vision of the future when women are in full control of that which is uniquely their own: the body.

In many parts of the world, where women are still struggling to define, in absolute terms, their inalienable and unabridged right to own their body and with that ownership the right to use it and present it how they wish, I believe this book of poetry is important artist contribution. Underpinned by a profound philosophical rationale with the concrete and tangible reality of a world in which women exist and still struggling toward a more perfect balance of personal choice and societal expectations, it is book of beautiful poetry.

Michael Linnard, CEO
New London, CT 2010

INTRODUCTION

LadyVishuss Poetics

She ran off and joined the circus. And, indeed, some women did. My Great-Aunt, Josephina DiMartino Capone, or, Josephine, as her name was Anglicized, became one of those women who followed her bliss. She left behind a husband and two children during the Great Depression to work as a snake charmer and bareback rider on the traveling circus and sideshow circuit. Of course, such a scandal caused Josephine to be ostracized from the family, so that to this day little is known of her life as a performer. She remains unforgotten in family folklore, however, and her decision to embrace a nontraditional lifestyle serves as the inspiration for the collection of poetry you now hold in your hands.

Apart from the shock of a woman not finding satisfaction in housekeeping and child-raising, society during the mid- to late- nineteenth-century took a dim view of circus women. They were considered little more than prostitutes, because they placed their bodies on display for money, regardless of the genuine skills involved in many of the acts. Plus, the unique amount of freedom afforded to women performers only added to the perception of promiscuity, realistic or not. A woman who participated in a sideshow, circus, theatre troupe, music hall, or vaudeville would struggle to regain entry into "polite society," as her morals would always remain circumspect.

Interestingly enough, at times the circus environment itself could model the prevailing culture's expectations for women. At the beginning of the twentieth-century, circus owners, in an attempt to market their performances as a respectable form of entertainment for families, would generate publicity articles that proclaimed the domestic interests of their top-billed female performers, occasionally noting that circus women were silent during their acts, unlike "bold" female burlesque performers. For example, Lillian Leitzel, considered by some to be the top circus performer of all time, was promoted as "committed to nursing injured animals" and "telling stories to small children" when not practicing her act.

The Ringling Bros. Circus insisted the female performers in their shows sign contracts with a separate list of rules for women that did not pertain to male performers, such as "you are required to be in the sleeping car and register your name not later than 11 p.m. and not to leave car after registering" and "be neat or modest in your appearance." These rules policing women were made public, so residents of local towns could feel confident that "Flappers" and free "New Women" would not be roaming their streets.

And yet--and yet--titillation was always a part of the circus promotional package. While promoting women performers' athletic skills and fresh out-of-doors complexion, handbills and posters highlighted the skimpy outfits and tights. Often, photographers, in an early form of photoshop, would replace a female circus performer's athletic muscles with the soft-curved body of a Ziegfeld Follies dancer. And then, of course, there was the sideshow.

Named for its location off the side of the midway, the sideshow served as the location for displaying human oddities: persons with disfigurements, and "fake" freaks, such as Spidora, headless women, fortune tellers, snake charmers, and other illusions/performances. Loosely touted as "educational," the sideshow became the location for some of the most exotic, and by extension, erotic, displays of the body, as women, many of them Euro-American women, dressed in provocative outfits in the guise of representing a racial or ethnic "Other." (This stereotype of ethnic "Other," much to my surprise, included Italian women also; this can be seen in Lulu Lataska's occasional respelling of her stage name as "La Tasca.") The idea being that only white women needed to be portrayed as wholesome and protected. Any other woman's body was fair sexual game. Big Top female performers were always referred to in promotional materials as circus "ladies," never as "girls," with the noted exceptions being the corps of Ballet Girls, and the less formal "statue girls." But the sideshow women were known as the "strange girls," a name self-selected or self-embraced. A name also that, to those outside the realm of traveling shows, encompassed all women within.

Body politics in poetics is a fairly recent phenomenon. Only since the 1960s, with the rise of the "second wave" of feminism, has the female poet claimed the right to write poems that delve into lives of women through the metaphor of the body; by daring to write the truth about women's lives. Anne Sexton, Adrienne Rich, and Lucille Clifton are just three poets who broke new ground in this area, and countless women poets have continued this tradition of personal poetic witness; as the "personal" very often becomes the "political."

Recently, in a lively discussion with several poets, after a reading that featured a well-known national poet, the concept of changes within the poetic landscape was debated. Poetry of confession and psychology was suggested to be no longer necessary; rather, it would be poetry that demonstrated how to navigate or circumvent the information age, commercialism, and the barrage of social and political upheavals that would be of the most use to contemporary audiences. This was the truth to which poets of today must speak. I do not disagree with this. However, I would argue that in a society that considers watching contestants lose weight, or people getting piercings or tattoos, or even the procedure of birth, forms of televised entertainment (once again under the guise, as in the sideshow, as "educational"), poetics that speaks to the body politic is both vital and valid.

Women cannot afford to lose--politically, economically-- the voice of the body. The history of women can often be viewed as the progressive march toward the ability to make their own choices, be it in marriage and home life, school and athletics, workplace and politics; and these choices are often centered around breaking past sexual taboos and reclaiming the body. From the choice to wear short skirts or bloomers or makeup, to equal access to athletics, to voting to enact laws against domestic violence and sexual harassment in the workplace, to serving in the military under combat, to birth control and abortion, to equality for women in the BLGT community, the body of woman is the battleground. Lessen the vigilance, allow ambivalence to seep in, and gains will be lost. Poetry of the body politic can not be allowed to be declared no longer necessary any more than feminism itself. If we enable literary culture, impacted by conservative political trends, to inform poets that the voice of the body is not needed, it will be a long haul before it is once again available to readers who need it most.

For me, then, what I term "LadyVishuss Poetics" is the dialogue that occurs in my own work between history and the contemporary, in relation to the body politic and ordinary women's lives. LadyVishuss Poetics aims to speak "truth to history," not to forget, but to add to, the historical record, and to place its relevancy in context for a contemporary audience. In this sense, LadyVishuss Poetics speaks "truth to power." LadyVishuss Poetics also embraces the woman poet as a freak, a social construct that has, sadly, not completely diminished over time. Women who engage in creative pursuits, especially if they also happen to be mothers and/or wives, will still find themselves battling against the perspective that their artistic endeavors are little more than hobbies. LadyVishuss Poetics acknowledges that women poets write to speak their own, vital, vivid truths. Lulu Lataska, the snake enchantress gracing the cover of this book, epitomizes the outsider: the Bohemian. She is a woman performer who does not merely hold a snake, but decorates herself with them, their danger, their poison, their proximity to death. Yet she emerges joyous, and it is clear to the viewer, the audience, that whatever invisible social boundaries or barriers she faced, she would triumph; because, like my Great-Aunt Josephine, she seized her opportunities, blazed her own path, and made choices. In this context, then, the poem "Lulu Lataska on the Cover" can serve as my "Ars Poetica."

Enough of pitching poetics like a sideshow barker. The ice is melting in the lemonade, the roasted peanuts are beginning to cool, and a line is forming in front of the ticket window. Ladies and gentlemen, poetry lovers of all ages...On with the show!!!

Joanie DiMartino, a.k.a. LadyVishuss
May 27, 2010, Under a Full Moon

"It is very, very funny to me, when I think of my smiling to the audiences as if it were real fun to charm the snakes, and all the time, I am bradding them and etherizing them and shaking in my skin for fear they will tighten their coils and be too much for me."

—*Lulu Lataska, Snake Enchantress,*
discussing how she would place a silk-lined pouch
containing an ether-soaked sponge in her corset
and sharp brads in her slippers before performances.
New York Daily Times, *April 19, 1891.*

Unidentified Lady Contortionist, c. late 1800s.
Photographer: Charles Eisenmann.

*

Calliope breathes

and this air
fills the calliope

laced with gold-leaf

then whistles through pipes
a joyous voice

above the circus parade

*

before the lady dainty
enters the ring

with a fang-bared tigress

the calliope's keys
must be teased

valves release steam

this honeyed melody
        heeded

Leg One

placing the skull in her hand

Unidentified Tattooed Woman. c. 1890s.
Photographer unknown.

Mermaid

The fin leaves her thighs
sticky with sweat,

melts talcum powder
into her skin

with flecks of green
that match her jaded eyes.

She is bored,
watching a swath of sun

glint light patterns
off each sequin disk,

a loveliness admired
only from a distance

like a mirage of sea
women taunting shipwrecked

sailors. Herself a siren,
luring coins

from men's pockets
as they enter the sideshow.

She strums the few chords
she knows on a polished harp,

sings a folk song
about Cape Cod Girls, and dreams

of Hollywood, of stars.
She will endure

this job only until California,
and while she knows she is bait,

she no longer blushes
when men nudge each other,

point at her and quip,
smells like fish.

Spidora Views Cave Art

She loves the imperfect legs:
the way one leg
is partially worn away by time,
and each a different length,
all eight asymmetric
on the spider's body.
And the slight bulbous curves
at each spider's 'foot,'
revealing the exact place
the cave artist's fingers
lifted from the wall
before once again
sketching.

And then the fat, rounded body,
with fangs, about to enjoy
the first of five ancient
insects: vague daubs of paint,
yet four-winged.

To her, the artist is female,
and she envisions a woman,
exhausted at day's end,
awaiting her man's
return from the hunt.
What she witnessed on a web
she paints, smoothes the image
over rough rock,
while firelight
flickers and her child slumbers.

The myth, the woman
as spider, has begun.

carousel in winter

this carved whimsy
with floating horses   swift
smooth-rumped
and mottled in snow
like thinly coated powdered
sugar   where leaping stallions tow
hollow sleighs
under a cold canopy
one hoof raised
teeth bared
heads in mid-toss   frozen
as echoes of organ oom-pah
music swirl around each wind-
blown snowflake
the bundled girl
impatient for this chill
to end   for gilded mirrors to glitter
without this wintry blizzard
for the circle
to wend

Lucia Zora Atop Snyder the Elephant

When the ponderous pachyderm rises
on hind legs, tamed by the beauty
who rides his ivory ~

two slivers of moon
in the misty hush of the Big Top,
        Lucia balances

barefoot on the husky ends of tusks;
her spangles glimmer,
smile hypnotizes: she coaxes

spectators into ovation,
        standing.

Portrait of a Young Woman as Poet

for Mosaic

Afterwards, she appraises
her own image in oils.

Her approval taut
as the rows of blonde curls
adorning her head,
or the front lacing of her burgundy
gown. The gown
rustles, leaves an echo
in the villa hallway;
a softness whispers along stone walls
like the shifting pages
of a partially-written book.

She wonders
at the brazenness of the painter,
placing the skull in her hand:
a headless woman
who cups her own mortality—
like peasant grotesques
at carnival
in a riot of colored ribbons,
wine merchants, and laughter.

She wonders too which will dry
faster, the paint on that canvas
or the ink
from her manuscript;
an opened book
shadowed in the portrait corner.

She does not need to wonder
which would be easier to burn.

Spidora Undergoes *Metamorphosis*

She insists on assisting in the creation
of her exhibit: the puppet spider
just so, with leg fur the correct shades
of grey and brown, and she dyes
her own hair a shock of black
to match the abdomen, starves
herself as though her diet
consisted solely of insects,
and hides her face
from the sun to stay pallid.
The rope webbing of softest Manila hemp
bleached to contrast the tarantula,
her curtains real silk, *and yes*, blood-
colored. The gaff steps
a greenish-rust, to evoke the rainforest
where intrepid explorers
first 'encountered' the grotesque.
She speaks incessantly
of immense tropical spiders
living alone, goliaths in guava trees,
and regales roustabouts with stories
of the deadly South American bird-spider,
Theraphosa blondii,
while she attaches the finishing detail
to the bottom step
of this box—her prized possession:
a preserved and desiccated
delicacy, a male crimson topaz
hummingbird.

Great-Aunt Josephine: Lost Photographs

I sift through pictures, seeking your eyes,
my own set jaw.

Bare-back on elephants you rode the Depression,
cotton candy dust clouds shimmered
over a deserted spouse—
two children.

Circus-sequined three rings sparkle: an allure
not found in two rings
and diapers.

Scandalized families destroy images;
leaving me to envision a woman with strength:
a fierce insistence to choose

and unchoose.

Isabelle Butler Rides *The Dip of Death*

The car is waiting.

Parked high above the arena, atop
serpent-shaped steel, the novel machine
sits in full view as a tiny brunette

ascends the platform and enters the car.
After signals given, she works levers, launches
down the steep incline, and rockets

across the open chasm in the track
                    upside-down!

like a meteor through galaxies.
The car's wheels churn space
until it again connects with the track;
when it slows, she alights.

The press call Isabelle a "skilled
automobilist."   She calls herself:

Daredevil.

The Tattooed Woman

She strips to painted skin,
lays among blossoms as rain-
washed dirt soothes
the newest pricks of spring;
colors rise to her surface
like wet petals:
this hyacinth, that tulip,
an early rose's thorns ~
a self-portrait in ink.

Spidora Polishes Her Toes

Her breath catches at the back
of her throat; she stops, peers deeper
into the pet store vivarium,
sure her eyes do not deceive her:
Such a darling spider!
The store owner lets her hold
the Guyana Pinktoe Tarantula,
and the spider prances
across her palms on little rosy toes.
She has never seen a spider
with this coloring: all black
and brown, with each toe-pad a dab
of soft pink, and although docile
in her hands she returns the spider
to the store owner, as she's not allowed
the pet.   But that night,
fresh from a steamy bath, she polishes
her own toes the color of orchid
petals in rain,
so that both she, and the Guyana
Tarantula, strut in blushing
Lady's Slippers.

When a Circus Troupe Kidnapped María Izquierdo

The room holds fantasia, with *Payasos*
in blue and yellow satin outfits
who make her giggle and clap her hands
when her glance strays to the door. They tumble,

perform somersaults and back flips,
and juggle orange and red and purple balls,

and feed her candies pulled
from shirt sleeves. When she slips
into that deep toddler slumber,
they return her to her weeping mother,

but the festive hues and stardust
sparkle ever after in her eyes.

Spidora Embroiders Her Words

```
        D                                    I
     I    E                              P    D
    P       R          web             S       E
   S                  venomspin                  R
        D            carapacefang          I
     I    E          nimbusspinneret    P    D
    P       R        eightpreyhuntjump  S       E
   S                 silkwidowhairyradius         R
        D            spiderlingmoltegg      I
     I    E          gossamer           P    D
    P       R          bite            S       E
   S                  arachnid                   R
        D             attacop                I
     I    E           iiiiiiii          P    D
    P       R          orb             S       E
   S                                             R
```

Aprile and Mae

two circus cherubs
frolic and flip   skip through antics
to the beat of a brass band
the debut of two new acrobats
brunette twins in a tandem act
in matching milky costumes with lemon
on shoes   hair ribbons   and fringe
one hugs juggling props in her arms
cradles citrus exotic as camels
to rubes washed with melted
icicles of a new spring
handed a sun-flecked orange by her twin
the sister tosses it to a hungry girl   who claws
into the sweet-fleshed fruit
the juice running down her chin   the rind
under her fingernails   outside the watery spotlight

Great-Aunt Josephine: Two-Way Mirror

A modern House of Mirrors,
with me illuminated,

holding a candle close to peer
at this body awash in wavy isinglass.

Two generations after your birth,
also divorced and shunned,

I scratch my nails
down the polished metal

of your circus
past, unable to dig deeper

as the hot wax stings my fingers
on my own chosen

Bohemian path.
On both sides of this mirror

stands a Strange Girl:

      I am your
Doppelganger.

Leg Two

out of myth, the brazen one

Zaluma Agra, Star of the East, 1875.
Photographer: Doane.

Mirth & Mayhem

One pulse of a circus: the hum of cotton candy
machines— Flaminia fancies how they mirror
cicadas, a steady drone in evenings before she performs.
And also when the barker cajoles from the midway:
Step into the sideshow! See the fire-breathing
man...the two-headed goat! All outside nature's balance!

An illusionist once stole a kiss, and she lost her balance.
She refuses blue tulle costumes, as the cotton candy
color reminds her of his mayhem: heated lies, fiery breath.
Now in mornings for luck she avoids mirrors,
and hides in crowds along the midway
between performances.

The Big Top captures mirth when aerial performers
soar into the canopy: a precise balance
of swing and release, with somersaults midway
to the next trapeze; Flaminia envisions clouds of cotton, a candy-
sweet conjuring, an illusion without mirrors.
In her flights there is no earth, and the fire-breathing

man warns her of no heaven—only that place with fire breathes.
She heard rumors from other strange girls who perform
from town to town (a rape in the House of Mirrors,
a slow arsenic poisoning by an unbalanced
clown). Sideshows sour souls like old cotton candy,
shriveled and bitter-stuck behind the midway.

Two acrobats juggle down the stretch of midway;
an audience holds its breath as fire
torches are flung like sticks of cotton candy.
From the back of the crowd, Flaminia admires the performers:
their skill, their balance.
Each man a mirror

of the other, the way the sideshow mirrors
the circus, a dark reflection of the midway,

a seedy counterbalance.
She notes the clown, illusionist, and fire-breather
deceive when they perform,
and desires innocence, melted like cotton candy.

The midway sparkles with merriment: a path mirrored
with light, cotton candy, shadows, and fire-breathers.
Each night she performs—a balance, a trapeze.

Mabel Stark Misses Her Tigers

On the third day after her mauling,
when doctors   still
would not let her leave
her bed,

the ballet girls
crept to her Pullman car window,
released hundreds of monarch
butterflies

to comfort her with a swash
of orange and black.

Spidora Finds Religion

Philosophy the First

she tries so hard
each day   to be

'above goodness'

to reach the Divine One

she imagines goodness
as linked concentric circles   like the web
of an orb spider

a gradual widening toward
perfection

Arachne, Mother of Spiders

The young girl was taught the story
of vain women

who weave,

who design their own destinies with fat spinnerets
full of silks and linens,

who painted flawless tapestries with skeins of threads
dyed with dried bodies of cochineal insects,

who spun myth out of history and then mystery
out of myth; and of the brazen one

who challenged a Goddess,

who afterwards in slumber found herself morphed
shriveled and shrunk, and yet

who dangled,   still so daringly,
from the silk of her own body.

Philosophy the Second

In secret
she begins to celebrate

the Octaves

first the Privileged
        then the Common
                later the Simple

On each Eighth Day

she lights a candle
        breaks bread
offers a prayer   *Blessing*

beasts with eight legs

The Solemnity

Alone in the library,
she reads early convent histories:
how each woman sequesters

anew in a stone web,
vows silence,
poverty, chastity,

and finds the strength
it takes to rise and spin the same quiet
patience as the day before.

Afraid herself to speak,
to break the hush she holds,
she only whispers their names:

Thecla   Hildegard
        Wulftrude

                Eufrosine
        Radegund   Sadalberga

each click and hiss against her tongue
alive in her mouth, and she repeats the archaic
sounds until they spill

like a liturgy
of chant, echoing inside chapel
walls. In paintings she sees

the dark habits
bulge unformed around their bodies,
and they resemble sated ticks

in summer woods.
Virgo Intacta, she reads,
Brides of Christ, but to the young

girl the nuns in black
are not brides but hungry widows:
they have not eaten; they have not mated.

Philosophy the Third

These are her bedtime stories

    anansesem
        anansesem

homespun tales
she dreams to herself
although slumber

balloons along the path of stars
    just out of reach

    anansesem
        anansesem

she honors   she names

    anansesem

Praise Song for Anansi's Wife

If she were to marry, it would only be to a man so
cunning he could convince the tiger to relinquish its
kill when she hungered, so shrewd he could hide her
from the python in the serpent's own lair, so clever he
could trick the stars into adorning her dress, bedeck
the lobes of her ears. Yet curled in grass patched with
yellow sun, twisting her hair around her finger as a
single ant roams the country of her foot while she
reads and re-reads Anansi stories, she is not so certain
she would embrace such a state at all. For what does
a woman trade in return for one so slick he spins silk
from his mouth?

Philosophy the Fourth

she was made of clay

shaped of ochre earth
into girl-child

her body soft   pliable
*   her will   yields*

to long days of rain
*   to moon rhythms*

to the unseen silver thread
*   connecting her to the sky*

in the dark purple light
of each dawn

Spider woman's gift

Brought home as a newborn,
      she envisions two aunts
           smoothing spider silk
                onto her tiny hands,
                    then the caress and rinse
              of warm water. This ensures
        like the women before her
      she will learn survival:
how weaving can clothe,

warm with blankets,
      create baskets to carry
           corn on journeys. No
                longer an infant, she yearns
                    for maturity, for days when
              her hands will find use
           in the steady repetition
      of threads along the loom,
in shedding, battening,

taking up the fell of warp
      and weft. She strives to live
           her life like new-spun
                wool fabric, connected
                    to shape a greater whole;
              but for now she curls
           under covers like a scorpion's
      tail, imagines slipping through
openings left for the Spirit.

Lament for Little Miss 1565

Your white dress shows smudges of mud
      and sawdust footprints from your trampling,
and your white skin exhibits shoe-shaped bruises
      in stunning purplish-black.

As your tender internal organs shut down,
      a sweet illusion of calm steals over
your tear-stained face, framed by blonde hair in disarray,
      slightly singed, like corn silk

in the height of summer. With your head cradled
      on a hospital pillow, unconscious, your dreams
billow up, and you drift back under the big top,
      but not the tent of parched paraffin flames

raining onto the panicked violence that separates
      mother and child; rather, this circus
opens with spangle-robed elephants that rumble past,
      single file, holding tails in trunks,

and pretty ladies on prancing horses with pink feathers
      in their hair. You stare wide-eyed
at the acrobats, the fearless woman riding a bicycle
      across the high wire, but you prefer

the clowns with big smiles and buckets of confetti,
      as your giggles peal out between bites
of cotton candy. You release your balloon into air
      when the trainer invites you to waltz

with her fringe-collared brown bear wearing a white
      satin party hat, and you dance together
in the spotlight inside the center ring
      until you rise above the animal cages,

up over bleachers, safe in the bear's arms
      as you sway past the trapeze and your yellow

balloon, while the bear twirls you higher,
    through the tent's deep blue

canvas roof toward the brilliant July sky;
    higher still you whirl, over the midway Ferris wheel
into cub-shaped clouds, heading up to the sparkling
    stars sculpting Ursa Minor.

Clown Psalm

Thalia, the Alley is no place to pray--
          --comediennes glide by on stilts
miniature cars zip through--
          --fresh footfalls, oversized red shoes
a harlequin weeps in the corner--

          --the Alley, Thalia, is no place to pray
yet cracked-paint smiles crave holy water--
          --from squirting daisy boutonnieres
and the manna of banana creme pies--
          --to quell spinning plates of hunger
which the jester heralds with bells--

          --no place to pray, Thalia, in this Alley,
with bold pink wigs stashed in trunks--
          --and rubber chickens await sacrifice
to You, Muse of Comedy--
          --by feather-clad fancies and mummers

the Alley prays, Thalia, this place--
          --where tramps prostrate with Pratt falls
in straw and sawdust--
          --and mimes who meditate
count prayers on linked scarves--
          --instead of beads or tumbled stones

this place, the Alley: it prays, Thalia--
          --for laughter's swells
taste the same on sinful tongues.

Evetta Matthews Clowns Around

In tights that show
the curve of calves,
the sleek flesh of thigh,
dyed the same rosy hue
of her sex between,

the lady jester
struts from the ring,
sits among men
on the south side
of the tent, and rejects
the ringmaster's offer
of $5 to return.

*These men here offered
me $10 to remain*, she
retorts, then crosses her
stockings, and lights
a cigar in the lurid
heat of spotlights.

Eve Eating a Candy Apple

just another strange girl
from the burlesque show,   costumed in fig
leaves   (and little else)

maybe she climbs

in and out
of boxes all evening,   her own rib cage
sawn in two at   each performance

maybe she charms

the hiss and slither
from bored, overfed snakes,   the men
again desirous,   back-room beguiled

instead,   far from the midway
Eve leans against an apple tree,   licks
    hardened sugar,
                    then crunches
through coating
the color of her painted cheeks
     sharp as glass shards

  these tart, glazed apples
bare their fruit flesh,   offer each town

a stained sweetness

Leg Three

such vile medicine to ingest

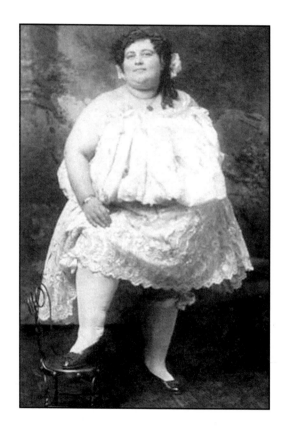

Unidentified Fat Lady, c. late 1800s.
Photographer: Frank Wendt.

Sword Swallower

The tawdry carnival tent's dark canvas
serves as perfect outdoor
backdrop

where the Albino Woman indulges
the photographer with this simple, stunning
act; a salacious flair

for swallowing steel. The billowy cotton shirt,
the red skirt trimmed in gold ribbons and sequins
swept to the left side of her body

from a steady breeze, caught by the camera's shutter.
She appears impaled by two swords:
a motionless

double cross, with arms outstretched,
head thrown back, thin silver blades and hilts
jutting from between her

parted lips. The tender curve of her throat
exposed to the lens like the white flesh of a sliced
ripened pear: open,   offered.

The Fat Lady Hums to Herself in Autumn

fifteen sixteen
chef's in the kitchen

October light thickens across the pasture
where the bull calves I'm weighed
against each circus run
graze under leaves
those flushed sideshow
banners announce the harvest

plump and ripened
me
a pumpkin

nineteen twenty
my plate is empty

I tire
of staring
at slim
women
through
withering
heat those
ladies
brittle
like dried
cornstalks

eyes
hollow
with denial

Katie Sandwina "Tosses Husband about like a Biscuit"

> *"I don't approve of women who paint and write. They should clean their houses and cook good meals. Will your stone cutting make you a better wife?"*
>
> *"Yes," replied Yandell. "I am making muscles. Then I can beat biscuit."*
>
> *--Julia Grant, wife of U. S. Grant, to renowned sculptor Enid Yandell*

Muscles bulge from her bare arms
like yeast-risen biscuits:

her short, tight bodysuit reveals a physique
the famed strongman Sandow competed against
      and lost,

relinquished his title
              Strongest Man on Earth!
his name thieved in taunt
or feasibly   honor,

that 300 lb. un-lifted barbell now a mere shadow
on a semi-darkened stage.

           *

But the center ring is all illumination
when Katie enters,
her husband heaved above

her head with one hand, dried crumbs
of unkneaded biscuit dough

on their kitchen floor, work left undone,
the oven yet unheated. While she sculpts her body
into Amazonian ideal

the Lady Hercules
wrestles her flexed reflection.

Popcorn Butcher

She craves the sultry
in the stirred heating of oil
and popcorn kernels,
their rushing *tinks* while poured
into the pot resemble a summer rain
from the drop of moisture deep within
each seed that swells into a Tommy gun
stutter as they explode
open and flow over the side of the pot
like shooting stars
trembling on the edge of sky.
The steam seen on glass walls
also dampens her skin as she scoops
the popped corn into bags, and a savory
aroma floats on night air,
teases the crowd with tentacles
as she pushes the red and gold
popcorn maker
among them, hawks salt and butter-
laden morsels kept warm by a light
that beckons like a beacon
to those already forming
a line.   The next morning
she rises before dawn, before bird song,
wipes the machine down,
cuts through grease on the glass
with a cloth doused in white vinegar,
empties the tray
of dud kernels and burnt hulls,
and replenishes the bags, butter, corn,
and salt shakers. She notices
spilled popcorn scattered
across the grass from the previous
evening: bags upset
by eager children, pieces dropped
by lovers feeding each other,

forgotten nibbles that slipped
through fingers, mouths, or were tossed
in the air by boys for sport;
these nubs sprinkle the landscape of the lot,
almost as though circus grounds blossom
random fields of Edelweiss. She smiles.

Spidora Identifies with Flies

Once, she craved the solitude
of autumn woods
to break open her heart
in the evening air.

Off the path, she noticed
an orb web cast between two
trees; the sticky net full
of winged catch.

Among the gnats and mosquitoes
were four common flies: two
lay prone, resigned to fate;
the third was missing a wing;

the fourth struggled against
silk robust as steel cable.
Engorged, the spider
squatted in the center,

un-phased by the fluttering
along the line.
She watched a while,
then stripped a twig of bark

and sliced through the portion
of web clutching the busy
fly. With prey released and web
still intact, she

walked on, sucking the spider
fibers from peeled tree
marrow: on her tongue the wood
smoother, softer, than bone.

Great-Aunt Josephine: Savory Gossip

They speak openly in the kitchen, amid bubbling
pots of tomato sauce and garlic, of how you left your family
that early morning in spring, after sending your children
off to school. The conversation sprinkled
with the word *putana*, like oregano in sauce, piquant.
Mixing veal and pork with bread crumbs and egg,
a cousin mentions again how you left
one last tray of manicotti in the oven, and voices lower
as they try to guess which man lured you
to his cellar, plied you with too much wine,
and an in-law wonders aloud if he holds your snakes
as they slip over your shoulders,
what salacious name you now call yourself,
and sordid giggles rise to the back of their throats
while an aging aunt dressed in all black
at the table chopping onions crosses herself,
prays *grazie* to the Holy Virgin that your mother,
Carmela, God-Rest-Her-Soul, did not live to see this.
Drying the dishes, an unmarried cousin insists if she
were beaten as much by a husband she too would leave,
until the aunt, her own mother, smacks the table
with her palm, then scolds her to hold her tongue,
reminds her that matrimony is a sacrament.
Another in-law waves steam away from boiling water
as she adds ziti, talks of pity for your children,
your daughter raised without a mother,
you, the sideshow slut
who left her name along with her wedding rings
on a husband's night table.
What will the nuns at school think, questions
a pregnant cousin kneading dough,
her apron covered in flour and ricotta.
The women chatter all at once,
while the little girl with your eyes who snuck
into the kitchen to steal pizzelle from the sideboard
crouches unnoticed in the corner and listens, wide-eyed,
neglecting the cookie crumbling in her hand.

Spidora Studies Spiderology

She turns pages in books so old
they couch cobwebs between covers;
pores over natural history to memorize
her spiderology. She absorbs

the words and sketches of medieval
eccentrics who observed little beasts
that eat their feasts on lace.

She pauses at an illustration
of a single large X
with fourteen tight concentric circles,
a primitive whitework,
quartered   *the whyte*
and pure webbe is very soverayne...
to be layde to a freshe wounde
for it stauncheth the blode

a *spynner* placed center:
the head, with only two-eyes and fangs,
its spherical abdomen
divided into tiles, and dotted,
like a turtle sunning on a rock   *it sitteth*
in the myddes of the webbe
redy to take suche flyes and vermin
as cometh in it

eight hairy legs jointed inward
resemble elbows and arms
more than legs, each
with three-pointed toes   *the spider*
hath many fete at leste VI
or VIII

But it's the cures for *venym*
that she finds most fascinating,

that later cause her to coax
spynners out of their *webbes*
and into her hands,

to cup and shake them
so they bite her repeatedly:

for it *is gode to be dronke with swete
wyne for the bitte of a spinner*

yes, she whispers over and over,
as her palms swell and redden
with the sting

of maddened arachnids, *it is gode
to be dronke
      with swete wyne*

An Appetite for Glass

To end,
I eat a bottle

of pale green glass,
with amber highlights

that sparkle onstage.
Men don't expect a geek

to know how to lick,
to take a bottle into the throat—

so when my tongue begins
to slide around the neck,

slip teasingly into the top,
you can see their mouths part,

almost feel heartbeats
quicken, breath shortened.

Until I bite—crash the tip between
my teeth, while shattered dreams

engulf my mouth
and a room of desire

turns to nausea:
and another delicious,

primal fear.
Most nights,

I don't even taste
the blood.

Spidora Orders Curds and Whey

Her mid-day meal consists of this dish.

She spoons up single curds, admires
how they never form the same shape, as wrapped
prey appear different, each one a supple
form along strands of web, and she imagines

the clabber as her own batch
of spun bugs: the gnats, mosquitoes,
flies, and even moths with wings white
as her bowl, as alabaster as these lumps

of coagulated proteins her tongue
presses against the roof of her mouth.
When finished with the silky curds, she sucks
whey through her teeth,
feeds on liquids, envisions rennin
as the venom that melts insects into viscous.

She overhears cooks at the pie wagon
call her Miss Muffet,

and she doesn't see the semblance,
can't conjure up the winter day bare branches
webbed the sky, when Patience Mouffet's
father frosted the stale piece of cake
with sugar and mashed spiders

procured from the house's dark corners.
The sweet crumbs to entice his fearful daughter,
sweaty and ill with the fever, to swallow
such vile medicine, to ingest
the pulp of common arachnids, to bid her:

eat.

Leg Four

like joy corrodes the veins

'Spidora' exhibit, c. late 1800s.
Photographer unknown.

Spidora Dances the *Tarantella*

Like spider pheromones on thread,
her *noir* silk scarf diffuses perfume,
and musk mingles with sweat
on her skin. When her palm
strikes the tambourine
little cymbals jingle and cling
while her body twirls circles: barefoot,
wild, frenzied.
She grows heady, breathless,
and as the music roils to crescendo
the glare of street lights
blurs into a white sun
like that afternoon when the spider
bit her among the tall grass,
the ghost of his smile in the heat,
before that sharp pain
like fangs spewed a burning venom—
and doesn't she know how poison,
like joy, corrodes the veins?
As the six-eight beat surges,
she dances her own clockwise-pattern
cure; yet next time, her design
will be less frantic: rather, she'll capture,
then consume.

Swarm

She
prefers the
young males the
worker bees who feast
fat on honey and grow
lethargic after they're smoked
an hour before each show the bee
charmer performs her waggle dance
only once in afternoons after the bees
have spent the morning coaxing nectar
into honey and the crowds are thick and
lazy with heat their own bodies abuzz with
sugar and the sweet delirium of an unclothed
summer sometimes a woman screams when she
releases the swarm from its frame on-stage the gasps
as the charmer sheds   her yellow cotton shirt
no bearded lady she   see a silken bee bikini
cover her breasts thin   straps of insect on her
shoulders where she put   pollen fine fabric circles
hiding her nipples under the lulled bees the rasp breathing of the
woman fainted in the mid-row as the turn-table off-stage pumps flight of
the bumble bee and she dances for herself spins amber honey into money

Spidora Rides the *Spider*

When she slips inside the cart
and the machine tilts as its legs rise into the air,
she gives herself over

to desperate drops and counter-clockwise turns.
She asks herself: what is a life
without the risk

       of dangling

in air, a suspension with tremors
—of spinning, spinning—
from a filament

as fine as spun luck?
The hurdy-gurdy music churns
from the carnival performance stage,
encircles her

as the whirls whip with abandon,
and the orange lights that blink
the contour of the curved mechanical legs

blur against a night
webbed with stars, and she is happiest
when she lets go for the ride,

happiest, while she spins.

organ grinder

the blind bear
pirouettes
in the dirty street

she churns the crank
and tinny music
pierces the air

late nights
behind canvas tents
tumble

from her hair
with the sawdust
extra

to add the bear
the carnival crowds
around vendors

in dusk   still early
to seek the fading summer
under her skirts

drowsy with dull
circles of her hand
and his spins   woman

and bear
peddle their wares
meat and bread

stave off hunger
the flask of vodka secure
against her thigh

Great-Aunt Josephine: Loose Ends

Crimson lipstick will go missing
from the purse of her aunt downstairs
cooking the Seven Fishes Supper
this Christmas Eve,
when the allure of red and green
together entice your daughter
too much, or maybe the balsam fir
incense hypnotizes, writhes out
of the little chimney like a serpent
charmed by subtle tunes played
on recorder, mingles
with the scent of anise and chocolate
from the kitchen. Upstairs,
alone in the locked bathroom,
she will dust her face alabaster
with talcum powder, smear
a clown smile across her lips,
lift her brother's jade toy snake
over her shoulders, and move her hips
in circles like the belly dancer
she once watched on the silver screen,
eyes closed, humming.

Spidora Sings to Spiders

It's not the grey heft of elephants,
      or the brown diamond patterns
along the giraffe's graceful neck;
      it's not the pink
of flamingoes, or the bold squawks of parrots;
      nor the strange horns adorning
the wildebeests, the ennui
      of the heated, sleeping leopard;

rather, it's the amphibian house—
      that dark, winding hall that finds
her smiling. She toddles past camouflaged
      snakes, the chambers of bats,
into the glass-case desert realm of smooth-bodied
      scorpions and fat, lazy tarantulas.
On tiptoes she peers into a display,
      mesmerized as four pairs of eyes

return her gaze. It will be years before she
      learns the words *arthropod* or *arachnid,*
and as the creature creeps toward her
      on curved hairy legs, she follows
a child's instinct, serenades the silent beast:
      dried up all the rain
and the itsy-bitsy spider
      a melody that resounds throughout

the alcove, echoing off each spider's
      framed habitat. Her hands
finish the fluttery patterns, and as her song
      dies away she turns, ready to once again
embrace the sunlight beaming from behind the exit
      doors, which creates
an illusion on glass like a sideshow Pepper's Ghost:
      her head upon the spider's body.

Bird Millman Does *The Charleston*

She dances brisk kick steps
high above New York City streets

where a jazz band performs
the popular strains

as crowds below join in:
partners, solos, the whole block

swells into a rhythmic ebb
and flow matching

the tight-wire dainty who sings
and shimmies and tosses

confetti with a grace
pigeons and sparrows envy.

Zazel Blasted Out of a Cannon

At ninety mph she arcs over a parade of zebras

      center-ring clowns feign swoons
as this silver satin-clad pearl
perfects a trifecta tumble
sails into the net

when she loosens her hair from her helmet

      applause explodes
into air heavy with the tang
of gunpowder

'Tiny' Kline as Tinker Bell

Before she flits over Cinderella's castle

she waits in filmy pink wings
that sparkle,

recalls the crude red tights
with fringe to accent tits and hips
for cooch shows fifty years ago,
amazed

at how tonight she soars toward
some crazy wished upon
star

and glistens among fireworks.

Leg Five

the gross unfortunate of dusk

Kate Arcaris in a knife-throwing act, 1890.
Photographer: Charles Eisenmann.

The Gilly Girls in Need

find us through the fortune-teller:
cloaked from carnival din by sequins,
shimmery veils, and the twisting smoke
of incense, alone with a drifting
gypsy woman who is other,
who is mother,
the truth sifts from their pretty
mouths into the crystal ball:
imminent, expected.
We dance a cooch show
into early hours, then slip away
along a dirt path thick with cigar
stink and littered with ash,
ignore propositions
we might agree to on an ordinary
night. These nights,
the girls meet us by a tree
or broken fence, guide us to doors
they feel most safe behind.
Skilled in pennyroyal and tansy tea,
we linger as they writhe and cry
while they expel the fetus,
then assist in staunching blood
that will seep into a mattress,
or straw pallet,
feed them sips of broth,
or chamomile.
Sometimes someone passes a hat
before we whisk ourselves
to the morning train, the next town.
We never call it *cherry pie*;
that just seems too cruel.

Spidora Pulls the Legs off Spiders

It's in the open air
  of a dewy morning that she
    finds the most.

Shadowed behind the barn—
  the old mule stables
    vacant,

cobwebbed. She
  finds them plump
    and blood-drunk from a long

night's feast
  of gnats, mosquitoes,
    the gross unfortunate of dusk.

Daddy Long-Leggers are her favorite,
  the way they trustingly crawl
    into her hand

before she plucks four fragile threads
  from the beige button-body.
    Two random legs remain

on each side, and she studies
  their wobbling,
    how they suffer

this stunned pain
  in silence, and she
    thinks she must

resemble them: voiceless,
  since she has no words yet
    for distress.

The mute sun
      shines brighter in the sky,
          burns the dew

off grass blades and dandelions.
      Bored with this game,
          she races off,

leaves each stumbling spider
      doomed
          to the bird's cuspate beak.

Mother named Corbin seems very fond of it

and what would you do

once the war ended
and the land   a double-scar of scorch and blood
the memory of crops burned to ash
still fresh

we needed food
we needed cows   some chickens
feed corn   rye for baking
we needed fabric
new quilts for winter
pairs of shoes for children's growing feet
and something extra set aside for the doctor
when the fevers come on

so yes

I took her in a wagon on to Allensville
and displayed her
to folks eager to call her *wonderful
monstrosity*
and   *four-legged baby!*
which I suppose is all she is to folks

but I hold her while she gurgles and giggles
        just a little child   really

and for 25 cts. a peek at her

*outer legs seem to be stout
but the inner ones are not active*

20 for me   5 for the man with the tent

when the good reverend
pays   stops to talk   I tell him
we will survive
next winter now   but this last day of May

I sense her weakening

Divine Woman

Dogs come
for the headless carcasses:
shrunken strays, themselves freaks
with healed-over scars,
bent tails, a lost limb, a limp.
They tear at chicken entrails tossed
from the geek's tent,
snarl and yelp at each other;
feathers coat
the ground like dirty
snow.

Madame Zova watches,
dressed in a faded silk kimono,
her face
cloaked in greasepaint. She augurs
for rubes, but no longer
foresees her own future in tea
leaves. Dashing out
her cigarette, she
turns toward the glittering
tent, shifts her pickled punk
on her hip; her plain
name on her lips
as stars gather
to gawk at a full moon.

Spidora Contemplates Children

Her apartment spills over with spider
plants. She admires the long blades

that curve over the sides of terra cotta.
Each with eighty-eight legs, she muses,

instead of eight. Come spring, they reproduce:
little spidery orbs, puffs of flora,

on lengthy tendrils that cascade
throughout the tiny rooms, blousing

back and forth in the heavy
breeze of early May afternoons:

wee beasties, she whispers,
cups them in her hands

and coddles the newborn sprouts
while she re-pots

them in rich soil. She longs
to swaddle her spiderlings

in silk, bind them womb-tight to her
through umbilical spinnerets,

smother each one until powerless
with succulent bruises, with puncture wounds.

Mrs. Sibilant's Splendid Hair Tonic

for Proper Moiselles and Ladies Who Enjoy the Refinement of
Womanly Hair Length

Those lasses pose their hair at each sideshow:
fair tresses unbound they hawk a cream
in pretty jars whose glass gleams green.
While mother drives the wagon over roads

her daughters brush and braid each other's
blonde coiffures, the manes of all three sweep
their feet. The flaxen trio bestows money
late at night, to mother's purse kept close;

after they tell town girls with bald desire
about techniques to wash and comb, then rub
elixir onto scalps. The sisters demonstrate

on damsels coaxed to part with precious dimes
and purchase beauty's glimmers of seduction—
afraid how mother's scissors lacerate.

Spidora Shuns Arachnophobia

"...according to Freud, the fear of the bite of a spider
represented the fear of punishment." --Paul Hillyard

Dusk.

As twilight steeps
her bedroom in shadows,
she stares at lace curtains: her dull, empty
doll-eyed stare
which sees, then un-sees,

then pulls bobbin-made patterns
into hazy effect, like the fine gauze
she longs to wrap herself in,

hide in silence

from the beatings,
the belted cat with nine tails
hand-bound to a used broom handle.

Following her punishment,
the child-choked sobs and bath-soaked welts,
the nine-tailed bully
will wait patient for the next infraction,
centered in her fractured home.

That night, awake, she vows
to stop counting at the number eight.

Little Accuracy

The knife thrower trains her daughter
by making her stand target.

She has known the *whizz*
and *thump* of the blade since birth,
but now must learn that crisis
of trust, find a true faith in aim.

Her mother wants to teach her
proper poise, how to keep icy still
and silent
before each pointed dagger.

Inside the practice tent,
arms extended,
the girl wiggles her dirty toes
in the sawdust on the floor,
holds the heavy summer

air in her lungs, and tries to push
her own skin
through earlier perforations
in the scarred
canvas.

Spidora Craves Attention

televisions   loom   in corners
spin channeled webs
          multi-eyed
she watches how it paralyzes
                    then drains
   life lust   from little sacs
         on the sofa
            and
she   longs to entertain
     she   aspires to be stared

           at

Leg Six

cropped locks and that curse

Mme. Fortune Clofullia, Bearded Lady, c. late 1800s.
Photographer: Charles Eisenmann.

Spidora Visits Mississippi

She fixates on palm trees: the way the leaves
                crown the trunk
like an arched spider, coconuts nestled beneath like eggs
                impatient to hatch.
Until she travels inland, and the cool breeze that breaks
                the late afternoon heat
into pieces sweeps under the Spanish moss draped over
                branches of live oak.

Her skin glistens with a humid film off the river, yet she
                stops frozen,
enamored of these cobwebs cast without spiders: a
                leisurely grey consisting
too of curved leaves, linked together like an elephant
                chain, that softens
as a sultry twilight approaches the landscape. The
                shadows creep forward

like a spider toward prey: slow, assured, and
                determined to feast
on what was once bathed in sunlight. The moss
                appears fragile,
like dust-laden web strands in a historic-house attic, that
                cradle echoes of once-
spoken words: the eight-score years of sibling arguments
                and a child's

fervent wishes, the rages and debates, the family scandals
                whispered, prayers
and supper blessings, laughter, the solemnity of deathbed
                promises forgotten:
those spaces in each life long-lost, long-hidden,
                long-ignored, tucked under
lids of chests, the bone-burying in closets, or,
                most likely, collected

as fine threads in an exquisite tortoise-shell hair receiver,
                                        then patiently weaved
and twisted, braided with a painter's shrewd eye into
                                        flower petals and leaves,
the subtle variations in hair color its own unique,
                                        multigenerational palette,
similar to the spider that never uses the same silk twice,
                                        so that all that's left

hangs in the corner gilt-framed, a form of beauty that
                                        only hints at the intricacies
of living, the way a torn, vacant web hints at caught
                                        butterflies, or how monuments
in a pristine field list single-file names, battle-wrought,
                                        unremembered. Now,
as she stands before a centuries-old oak with grey vines
                                        that cascade into a breeze-

filled twilight, her diaries destroyed, letters burned in an
                                        urn that holds the ashes
of greetings and gossip, her own human history, she vows
                                        herself to the sideshow,
if only to return here yearly to disappear among the
                                        shadows caused by cobwebs
of blossoming gossamer, these haunted ruins her winter
                                        quarters, her gothic nimbus.

inside the funhouse

and the rooms will change   and the floors
will move   and the book you put down
will not be there when you return   the alcoholic
on the second floor masquerades
as a cigarette girl   she will steal your meats
your expensive bourbon   make the lights
go out at random
while her lover plays the roustabout
taking odd jobs to sleep in her chamber
the squeak of mattress springs
a ceaseless   off-key lullaby
avoid the wild-haired clown
with black stockings
too-high heels   garish nails   and tatty lace
popping from her low-cut bosom
she will demand a quick fix
along with rent   for her wronged life
with talk of astrology   angels   and auras
Unbidden water   will pour and pour
through the pipes   until it soaks the rug
of the room you inhabit
seek another wall
for your photos than the one where you first
hung them   beware the untrained dog
with treat-lured jaws that chew and chew
the mechanical parrot squawking
big closets! big closets!
and the silverware that slips from drawer
to drawer like spinning spirals

                    but outside
oh   there is the warmth of summer nights
when you recall first sight
of the front door   and the gnarled hand of a crone
with candy house   holding out to you
        a caramel apple

Spidora Saves Spiders

Don't worry, spiders,
I keep house
casually.

Issa

Frenetic, her landlady cleans
and cleans,

insists the scrubbing of the tub
upon the shower's end,

beds made behind closed doors,
plates washed after the last swallow.

The landlady's mass of wild curls
trembles as she stamps out spider-life,

removes all traces of webbing,
lest the plumber notice lint

among the leaks. Yet she, our heroine,
rebels, in secret refuses

to vacuum a single corner of the closet,
where dust gathers in the strands

of gossamer, where common brown
spiders can be safely

apprehended with cardboard and spoon,
then released into a cloud-covered

morn while she whispers
encouragement.

why the two-headed juggler is female

first
name each ball

children   husband   career
household   hobby

then launch them
into the air that surrounds your heads
a split-second catch and care
before you reshuffle
prozac-ed pinks and yellows
and smile through eyes
jaundiced with exhaustion
while you pedal
a unicycle high-heeled
maintain balance
(and a cinch-waist leggy
beauty standard)
the years spin
like two wheels
nurtured
into constant
m o t i o n

Highwire Haiku

from the high wire
she knows distance is the same:
falling left or right.

heel to toe
the wire's cold tension
brands her bare feet.

circus scents of
scat and sawdust ~
she inhales/exhales
    inhales/exhales.

wobbling—
gasps from the audience
fill the canvas eaves.

sweat droplets
tingle her upper lip:
tongue (fear) salt.

her powdered palms
and a polished pine wood bar—
b a l a n c e

spotlights
weave between each step ~
her eyes unfocused.

the end platform
shimmers   a mirage
out of   reach.

sleight-of-hand

for h.r.c.

and still the woman
must step back   wait her turn
in curtained wings   prance
around on the national stage
like a fringe-dressed assistant
hawk the magician's skills
his merits   his bravado
even though she knows
the secret behind each trick
even taught him new ones
to polish his repertoire
and still   she flashes a stage-smile
and claps   leads the audience
in applause   she honors
the call *step down! step down!*
as the young magician
refines his act   and bows
and bows   and bows

Two Bearded Ladies

The lady with a beard
donned trousers,
a waistcoat and pocket watch,
and attempted to join the Army,
to 'beat back the Huns,' as the posters
urged, to help win the Great War.
She got as far as the medical board
before accepting defeat:
this was not her grandmother's time,
her grandmother's war,
where a man's costume,
cropped locks, and that curse
of facial hair on the family's women
resulted in enlistment:
one blue uniform and rifle
to shoot grey-coated Rebels,
a succession of military paychecks,
and tales to spin by a winter's fire
as granddaughters practiced
their stitching.

So instead,
the lady with a beard
once again cinched her waist
with a corset, grew back and curled
her brunette tresses, and signed
on to a traveling sideshow,
where vibrant banners now display her
as a demure pariah,
a bustled and bearded New Woman
eager to squelch all differences
between the male and female spheres:
Wants to Work...Wants to VOTE!
　　　　She sits on the edge of a velvet chair
above the audience and sighs at the irony
of that banner, this parlor-set stage
her workplace, and answers

questions about changing the Constitution
to give women the vote.
The same Constitution, she reminds herself,
that she, like her grandmother,
would willingly die for.

Josie DeMott Robinson Attends a Rally

It rained for days,
so when she rides her Lipizzaner
bareback out of overcast gloom,
her gold watered-silks
a new-washed sun,
and her purple sash a bold
lilac in bloom,
the women cheer,
wave banners,
and sing suffrage songs.
She commands the horse to rear up,
and newspaper photographers
snap photos of Josie posed
with one arm stretched,
her gloveless hand
holds the flash bulb-
brightened sky.

Leg Seven

fits of wakefulness
when her lust is slaked

Lulu Lataska in tights and short costume,
c. late 1800s.
Photographer: Charles Eisenmann.

Spidora Covets Silk Stockings

She obsesses over the caress
of spider silk
along the length of her leg:

such lustrous stockings!
Stronger and smoother than silk
from mere worms,

and she would wear
them better than any eighteenth-
century royalty

that received them
as novelties, after *L'Academie*
examined the threads,

considered costs. She would tie
them on her thighs
with red ribbons, and not hide

beauty under fabric,
but rather, remain naked
except for her silks,

and as she strokes her calves
with gossamer
from the grass of a dewy

morn, she imagines
rough hands
sliding those stockings down.

After Colette Performs *The Flesh* Outside of Paris

She agrees to receive the police
as an aristocrat of the stage:

kimonoed,   alone
in her dressing-room,
which reeks of ammonia
and wilted daisies
in a vase. She'll admit
the scene was banned:

ripped bodice, bared breast
and thigh, and she'll answer
all their questions
in beloved pantomime.

Burning Ballerina!

from the Penny Gazette

The skirt above her calves teased flames flickering in the footlights, bluish halos lining the music hall stage Thursday evening like bright will-o-the-wisps. A haunted glimmering of filmy stockings, ballet shoes en Pointe, and her own slenderness: bare arms and neck, the scooped leotard offering up her breasts; she danced like a ghostly silhouette against the backdrop of black stage curtains and the haze of smoke from cigars, from gaslights. Violin strains washed over the hall when the line of ballet girls twirled too closely to the cupped fires—and she was bliss, pas de seul as gossamer yielded to the rich silk of blaze.

The hero—or shall we say heroine—of the day was our own Miss Julia Dinsforth, of 9 Rose Street. A brave girl, Miss Dinsforth had the calmness of mind, so unusual for her sex, to locate a bucket of ice water backstage amid the pitched screams of both actors and audience, and doused the unfortunate ballerina before her body was ravished with blistering burns.

The ballet girl, known only as Russian Irinia, was taken to Dr. Nettle's infirmary, where the condition of her once-pale skin remains a mystery. Mr. DeWitt, sole owner of the DeWitt & Ripley Traveling Music Company, was nowhere to be found after this near-tragedy.

Youthful Miss Dinsforth will be receiving guests in her parlor this Tuesday at 6 p.m. to recount her harrowing tale: "to tell how I was there, how I even forgot the thick layer of October frost against the earth while walking home, the heat from her...so seared into my–"

Spidora Purchases Pumps

*"I wish you were an arachnid, so I could
buy shoes for all your feet!"*   —T. R.

She is patient, although indecisive,
tenderly removing the red
stilettos—again,
to model the black ones. A grim
shine flickers from them
in the mirror as she paces,
treads the worn store floor
like something captive, anxious.
She knows she is late,
but can't remember the obligation,
the location, or to whom it mattered.
For her, there is only here and now,
and the steady sex-click
of each pair of four-inch tapered heels
on wood. The color choice
reminds her of a roulette wheel,
of the silvery web spacing
the rouge, the noir,
each number a plump bug
spinning into its own ill-luck.
Always bet red, she once heard,
yet hesitates to gamble
against the shade of late
night, a time
when desire's thin lines set traps
and the winners, who survive,
are nocturnal.
Instead, she selects balance,
that slim place in the hourglass
when grains of sand
on both sides are
even, making her own odds
within a house
that is ultimately fixed.
She exits the store
with two pairs of each hue.

Great-Aunt Josephine: Anguine Hours

Λ woman slithers away
from identity, a shedding
serpent:

-woman, -enchantress,
    -charmer,
        -whore ~

in winter, bored, you
once spelled your married name
on an unmade bed

$c - a - p - o - n - e$

with the discarded skin
of your snakes.

A Treatise on Handling Snakes

"they shall take up serpents"
Mark 16:18

Some nights she slumbers with serpents, cold and coiled
against her ankles. The sloughing of dead skins,
the musk from her sweat-drenched and cum-soiled
sheets, offer *yes*, little salvation from Pentecostal sins.

In fits of wakefulness, when her lust is slaked
through this *yes*, distilled essence of the Holy Kiss,
erotic as this progression of her chosen snakes,
passing one town, two towns, the hiss

of the slowing train, itself a steel ophidian that curves
around mountains, into tunnels toward the next show,
the next stage, and the closing *yes*, velvet curtains
of a summer spent caressing naked heads of pythons, of boas,

of asps. She has found *yes*, sanctification mingled in semen;
milks the fangs each day of their viperous poison.

Spidora Receives a String of Pearls

"The harmless dewdrops, beaded thin,/
Ripple along thy ropes of sin."
--John Leicester Warren, Lord de Tabley

She could measure them
to the millimeter,
the little seed pearls
of silky nacre,
compare their width
to dew drops
gracing the orb-web

—both she,
and the spider, opulent—

after a night shrouded
by rain.

Making Jenny Haniver

These Jennys will give head to the Devil
if given half a chance, suck semen
reminiscent of Arctic waters: salt-laden,
icy. Little parted devilfish, spread
open and pinned to plywood,
exhibited far from the erotic
phosphorescence of the deep,
diffusing the soft pungent scent
of moist mollusks, littleneck clams
drenched in foam. Once
a dead sperm whale washed on a beach
the watery morning after a pounding
storm, the carcass hauled onto a railcar
and displayed to hinterland yokels
until the stench of rotting blubber
drove away more rubes than it drew.
Now, the bones and teeth, boiled
and bleached, collect dust
in faded winter light among these fake
mermaids in a dime museum, where a hand-
painted sign reads 'thar she blows!'

Lulu Lataska on the Cover

This mistress of the serpentine
in her wispy outfit
delights in gypsy tassels

of vivid pink and silver,
and the risqué
filmy fabric which barely veils

her thighs, her calves, down
to the laced-up leather
ankle boots,

her silken slippers
saved for low-lit sideshow
stages. But it's the boas--

not the bodice--
that complete the ensemble:
the arrowheaded

constrictors slither
sinuous over her pelvis;
forked tongues flicker,

sense her heat.
Unetherized, the boas
and pythons constrict less

than the fence across her
quim, and she raises
them writhing and coiled

above her nude arm,
the chain-links open for snakes
to slink through toward

the other side of train tracks,
the way an artful woman
will slip between two covers.

Leg Eight

each night behind closed blinds

Unidentified Statue Girls, 1903.
Photographer unknown.

Spidora Defies Description

a found poem

Hideous!
        Repulsive!
                Disgusting!

What does she eat?   How does she live?

She survives in total misery, for no man
can ever love her!

Yet she's...   ALIVE!!!

To praise the spider as I ought,
I shall first set before you the riches of *her* body:

Nature had appointed not only to make *her* round
like the Heavens,
but with rays like the stars,
as if they were alive.

The skin of *her* is so soft, smooth,
polished and neat, that she precedes the softest
skind Mayds,
and the daintiest and most beautiful
strumpets.
She hath fingers
that the most gallant virgins
desire to have theirs like them, long, slender,
round, of exact feeling,
that there is no man, not any creature
that can compare with her.

Who would not admire so great a force,
so sharp and hard bitings,

and almost incredible strength
in so small a body?

You won't   BELIEVE   your eyes!

Greasepaint Graces

I.   Mathilda

"A wind has come and gone, taking apart the mind...
How privileged you are, to be still passionately/clinging
to what you love..."

a winter without snow is like a drought

   i am parched ground without him   i know
where he winters
    when the circus season's over

   and i watch his apartment   count   the girls   entering\leaving
  time how long each stays   i know their names
     other statue girls

who spend their sweaty summers
       slicked with silver grease
  posed

    their nakedness barely draped
     to lure rubes
       through midways   into tents

   i miss
how he'd whisper mathilda as though i had a name that mattered
    how he'd rub
    my muscles ached with stillness   and still

      i will not quit the outskirts
  of his life
      this incessant drip of icicles

    girls invited to his door   unhinged

i sniff his pillow
     listen for the lift of his foot

   on the stairs

II.   Petunia   *23 fragments of a found poem*

> *"But ignorance//cannot will knowledge. Ignorance/wills
> something imagined, which it believes exists."*

hescancelledAGAINhescancelled   i went to his trailer uninvited
spent a night   alone in his   bed   waitingforhim to come home
hesbeengone four days   already   *i spent another tearful sleepless
night*   away from me   away from the act   away from practice   away
from   his sweet Petey   *i vow to help you grow into the man and
entertainer you want to be*   me   he's replacing me   that new
statue girl all youth and curves   she shows up one day like fresh dew
in a mauve sunrise   *i'm trying to get the tickets—maybe we can get
a room*   but i was first   besides   our passion could not be denied
*i know about Wednesday, what you did on Wednesday, who you
were with*   i need him in the act   in my life   i won't be a statue girl
forever   *i asked you if she's your one true love and you denied it*   i
won't be alone   he's my one   last best chance for happiness   *i've
begged you and begged you to be faithful to her*   and yet i spread
my legs for him   overandover   he always comes back to his Petey
and he's so good with his hands   *you're the only man i've ever
given goosebumps to*   why he doesn't juggle for hire each season i
don't know   *i know you're there for her, just like you were for me
and my surgery...i'm not mad*   but he's perfect for the act   he's so
perfect so natural   *i'm nauseous...i need this like i need a third
head*   he never asked   how i felt   how i would stay in the act with a
baby   his baby   i wanted his baby   *i don't think i can do the show
this summer if you're with her*   i wanted him to choose   he refused
*i can't continue sleeping with you while you're still sleeping with
her*   and i pretend pregnancy to win him   *i do love you, i do, i do,
i do love you, you know*   forgot a barker is never a mark   *i asked
you what was apparently a stupid question the other day, given
your actions*   i can't do this anymore ican't ican't ican't   yesterday
i snuck into his trailer it was easy   he's always with her anymore
ripped up her letters notfromme   stole her jewelry   notmine
TELL ALLEGRA SHE WON   chucked anything notme notme   her
notme Petey   *we were supposed to go to dinner tonight—i won't
be stood up any more*   after all   i'm a professional performer   too
a circus life with nights of bright lights   *i'm a nervous wreck trying
to please you*   a lady painted in stone-gray shades of day makeup
i've got my dress   i remember once my mother had a canary   it

sang so sweet   *i understand if she comes first*   for such a little bird
just lovely voice   *i do trust you*   song that evaporated into air   like
early silver morning mist   on daffodils   *i can't keep waiting for
the dust to settle over her*   but i have no song   a statue girl is silent
let's face it, i've been at your beck and call since September 1906
someday i want   *are you still in the act??*   to make music   sweet
like a canary   *i'd like to take you to your favorite spot for coffee*
someday i'll learn to play the flute

III.   Allegra

"Then you're in the world again./At night,
on a cold hill,/taking the telescope apart.//You
realize afterward/not that the image is false/but
the relation is false."

late one night I was shivering
          after a show   the cold rain

he threw his coat over my shoulders
          as I walked back

he didn't know at first   how I love rain
          he offered me coffee

thick with goat's milk, steaming,
          spiked with dark rum

of course I shared his bed that night
          and many nights after

we were playacting: he, a Pygmalion
          surrounded by statue girls

he'd woo with presents and words
          of wedding

some sideshow barker's silver-tongued
          lines   (but I was surprised

the way those girls believed
          his lies)

and I, an ivory-sculpted Galatea
          in love with   *Alive!*

scribed on shiny banners
          tied to nails on barns outside

before we'd arrive   at each town
        announced by screech

of train on rails   the way freedom
        sounds while the trees

are still green smears   viewed
        from a railcar window

but now the leaves are turning
        the color of wine

in a glass: some pale gold,
        others plum-red

and next year I signed to ride horses
        instead.

Great-Aunt Josephine: First Lesson

You can see the mare's breath
in a morning crisp
with dried leaves scattered
like roasted peanut hulls after a show,
her coat the same color brown,
only shiny in this watery
autumn dawn. You stroke
her muzzle, talk softly, offer sugar
cubes. Here to discover
each other's temperaments
so you may meld your torso
to the mare's bare back
like a glittery Centauridies,
you whisper how cramped places
make you skittish, recall
kitchenettes sized like horse stalls,
how one summer night
you bolted toward a grass field
dotted with circus tents to shake
out your hair under dark canvas
gleaming with stars, how you, too,
bristle under restraints,
be they leather   or silk.

'Marvelous May' Wirth Somersaults Forward

May leaps with her feet in baskets
from the ground
onto the horse's rump
while the mare thunders the circle
of the ring for the grande finale.
The crowd is avid, captive
to the rhythmic rush of hooves
as May propels herself
toward the sorrel's withers
in a somersault, and completes
the act standing in that place of perfect
balance on the mare's back,
the baskets' weave unmarred.
As she curtseys, May's
signature pink bow
graces her own bobbed mane.

Why Mata Hari Leaves the Circus

She refuses to speak of dreams that haunted her
each night after shows; how through the diaphanous veil
of sleep the night mare would gallop

into the ring of her mind, chase the spangled horse
she rode in unison with seven other showgirls
until she could sense her horse break
from the line, crash a shin into the barrier
lining the hippodrome, bone
protruding, blood
speckled over sawdust,
courses down the length of the hoof.

In the next frame, she runs in slow motion
through a vapor at the eye of day
toward the lame horse
encircled by uniformed men with rifles.

She has just time from a distance
to blow the mare a kiss.

Contortionist

She enters the wooden
box with blown kiss,
hip shimmy. Her pale arm
waves at clusters of pasty
faces through a small side
window; the top sealed.
With a flat sword,
the magician pierces the box.
She screams,
and her bead-fringed dress
is thrown from the box.
Repeated, she relinquishes hose,
a girdle, lace panties.

*10 cents more to see her
without clothes.*

The titillation melts away
with each paid peek:
she is not naked.
Contorted against knife
blades in a flesh-colored
leotard, she wonders which
rube performs this scene
each night behind closed blinds,
who mingles arousal
with brutality, what small town
feed-sack dresses hide.

Sometimes, when she leaves
the box, there's a red welt
on her cheek, a yellowing
bruise on her thigh.

Divorcing the Strong Man

the never retrieved
beads he

cleaved from her neck

clattered to the floor
       scattered

beneath the chest
of drawers

As Lillian Leitzel Reaches 249

Only the air is dizzy, not Leitzel,
as she morphs into a luminous
human pinwheel, throwing
her sequined body over her wrist
again and again in the spotlight.

The audience chants each number
of her revolution, those one-arm planges
that dislocate her shoulder:

246... 247... 248... 249!

And the crowd's roar deafens
the petite performer,
a diamond
glittering on a ring.

Spidora Embraces Widowhood

She reminisces about her lovers
as a spider might dream of the gorgeous
butterflies ensnared:
a flash of frenetic fluttering in indigo,
crimson, or orange, or how violet softens
in a dying slant of sunlight
across the rumpled bed, his spent cock
like a crush-spun of antennae,
flaccid, silken.

For so long she has lived in the space
between the webbing,
                          solitary
except those moments,
too fleeting, when body encounters body
to mate, to eat, and she grows wistful
for the day when air lacks butterflies,
and electric bulbs along steel
no longer illuminate darkness with color,
and webs, pliant and torn,
crumble under the weight
of breeze-blown pollen, of dust.

She watches roustabouts
dismantle the ferris wheel, and she
likens it to disrobing—shiny carts removed
transform into semi-precious stones
unhooked from earlobes, and detached
metal poles in their faded piles
of grey become the cast-off clothing
with which lives construct themselves ~
so that only air is left,
and skin.

Millie Irene, trapeze artist, 1885.
Photographer: Wood

*

the woman on the platform clutches
a one-way ticket

for the 1:13 a.m. train to Sarasota

from heated asphalt streets that hold
echoes of her hurried steps

    steam rises

*

the woman hands the conductor
her ticket   her valise

finds an empty compartment

then   like the train releases steam
before it lurches from the station

    she releases breath

BIBLIOGRAPHY

The following works were most useful in writing this book of poems; however, this list is by no means exhaustive or representative of the total research completed.

Bogdan, Frank. *Freak Show: Presenting Human Oddities for Amusement and Profit. Chicago*: The University of Chicago Press, 1988.

Davis, Janet M. *The Circus Age: Culture and Society Under the Big Top.* Chapel Hill: The University of North Carolina Press, 2002. In particular, Chapter Four, "Respectable Female Nudity," pp. 82-141.

Fox, Charles Philip. *A Ticket to the Circus: The Stupendous Story of the Incredible Ringlings in all it's Amazing Detail from Humble Wisconsin Beginnings to World-Wide Glory.* New York: Bramhall House, 1959.

Hillyard, Paul. *The Book of the Spider: From Arachnophobia to the Love of Spiders.* London: Hutchinson, division of Random House, UK, 1994.

Nickell, Joe. *Secrets of the Sideshows.* Lexington: The University Press of Kentucky, 2005.

Piepmeier, Alison. *Out in Public: Configurations of Women's Bodies in 19th Century America.* Chapel Hill: The University of North Carolina Press, 2004.

Tait, Peta. *Circus Bodies: Cultural Identity in Aerial Performance.* London: Routledge Press: 2005. Also, the author's Keynote Address, "Circus Bodies Defy the Risk of Falling" presented at the Fabulous Risk Conference, December, 2006.

"The Hartford Circus Fire 1944" documentary; produced by Connecticut Public Television.

Nature books on spiders; websites and books on snake-handling rituals and spider-related mythology and folklore; websites and personal accounts of the Hartford Circus Fire; numerous circus-related websites, memoirs, journal articles, and biographies on specific circus performers; as well as materials related to music hall dancers and other artistic women.

NOTES ON INDIVIDUAL POEMS

Invocation

Calliope (pronounced cal eye' o pee) is the Muse of Epic Poetry. Ancient Greek poetry texts would often begin with an Invocation to the Muse, giving thanks for inspiring the poems within. A calliope (pronounced cal' ee ope) is a steam piano that would bring up the rear of a circus parade. Music from a calliope could be heard up to five miles away.

Leg One: *placing the skull in her hand*

Spidora Views Cave Art: poem is based on the earliest known artistic rendering of a spider, which appears on a cave wall in Gasulla Gorge, Castellon, Spain. "Spidora" is a sideshow illusion where trick mirrors are used to give the appearance of a live woman's head on a puppet spider's body, promoted as 'half-woman, half-spider.'

Lucia Zora Atop Snyder the Elephant: known as the "Elephant Empress," Zora was an animal trainer who oversaw the elephants in the Sells-Floto Circus from 1909-1917. Her most spectacular act was riding the tusks of Snyder, "the killer elephant" as he rose on his hind legs.

Portrait of a Young Woman as Poet: poem is based on the painting *Portrait of a Young Woman* (1574) by Paolo Veronese (1528--April 19, 1588). Born in Verona, Italy, Veronese became well-known for his frescos and oils in Venice, becoming one of the pre-eminent painters of the late Italian Renaissance. This painting hangs in the J. B. Speed Art Museum in Louisville, Kentucky, with a curator note informing the viewer that the symbol of the open book denotes a writer, and the skull her vanity and mortality.

Spidora Undergoes *Metamorphosis*: poem takes its name from 17th-century German painter and naturalist Maria Sibylla Merian's *Metamorphosis of the Insects of Suriname* (Amsterdam, 1705). Merian (1647--1717) was known for her work with caterpillars and insects, and her *Metamorphosis* was one of the first naturalist books on South American insect life. This work also includes a plate (18) featuring spiders and ants on a guava tree. A 'gaff' is a sideshow term for fake. 'Roustabouts' are general laborers in the circus. *Theraphosa blondii* is the current Latin name for the South American bird-spider, the largest living tarantula, which grows to the size of a dinner plate. It is known to prey on birds on rare occasions.

Isabelle Butler Rides *The Dip of Death*: Isabelle Bulter performed 'The Dip of Death' twice daily for the Barnum & Bailey Circus. She was also known as a trick bicycle rider. Little is known of her outside of her willingness to attempt difficult circus stunts.

When a Circus Troupe Kidnapped María Izquierdo: Mexican painter María Izquierdo (1902--1955) was popular in the 1920s and 1930s. She often portrayed women of the circus, claiming in her memoirs that this inspiration came from a brief kidnapping by a circus group that occurred when she was just two years old. A *Payaso* is a Mexican clown.

Aprile and Mae: poem is based on the painting *Jugglers at the Cirque de Fernando* (1879), a painting by Pierre-Auguste Renoir (February 25, 1841--December 3, 1919). Born in Limoges, Haute-Vienne, France, Renoir became a leading painter of the Impressionist movement.

Leg Two: *out of myth, the brazen one*

Mabel Stark Misses Her Tigers: the premiere female tiger trainer of the 20th century, Mabel Stark (stage name; born Mary Haynie, in Princeton, KY; date unknown) endured many maulings throughout her colorful career. She first joined the Parker Carnival as a sideshow dancer, and moved around to different circuses including the Al G. Barnes Circus while rising through the ranks, eventually becoming the best-known cat act in American circuses with the Ringling Bros. and Barnum & Bailey Circus until they decided to end cat acts in 1925. She committed suicide in 1968.

Spidora Finds Religion: the inspiration for this sequence of poems came from the many mythological/religious traditions that feature spiders. Some poems in this sequence draw directly from spider-related myth; others present a view of myth or religious philosophy with spider/arachnid metaphor.

Philosophy the First: is inspired by Neo-Platonism, the modern term for a school of religious and mystical philosophy that took shape in the 3rd century CE. Founded by Plotinus, it is based on the teachings of Plato and earlier Platonists, which believed in the primeval Source of Being as the One, and Infinite.

Arachne, Mother of Spiders: refers to the Greek myth of Arachne, the prideful young woman who challenged the Goddess Athena, Patroness of Weaving, to a weaving contest, which culminated in Athena transforming Arachne into the first spider.

Philosophy the Second and *The Solemnity*: refer to the near-defunct practice of celebrating Octaves (the eighth day after a religious holiday) within the Roman Catholic Church.

Philosophy the Third and *Praise Song for Anansi's Wife:* is based on 'anansesem,' which literally means 'the spider story' from the mythology of the Akan people of Ghana, West Africa. These 'spider stories' are where the popular 'Anansi' fables derived. 'Anansi' the trickster spider is one of the most important characters in West African oral tradition and folklore. Anansi's wife is not known by any particular name; she goes by several depending on the culture of the storyteller. A 'Praise Song' is a laudatory poem that captures the essence of the object, person, or god being praised. It is one of the most widely used poetic forms in Africa.

Philosophy the Fourth and *Spider Woman's Gift*: are inspired by the Navajo legend of Spider Woman.

Lament for Little Miss 1565: on July 6, 1944, the canvas of the big top at a Ringling Bros. and Barnum & Bailey Circus caught fire in Hartford, Connecticut, killing 168 patrons, many were children. "Little Miss 1565" is the name and number given to an unidentified young girl who succumbed to her injuries at the hospital later that day. Special thanks to Steve Taylor, survivor of the fire, for first bringing this tragedy to my attention, and for sharing his memory of that fateful day with me.

Clown Psalm: Thalia is the Muse of Comedy.

Evetta Matthews Clowns Around: Evetta Matthews was the first female clown, known for shocking crowds when she wore pink tights. She was an acrobatic English "lady clown," who embraced bloomers and the idea of the New Woman. She performed with the Barnum & Bailey Circus in 1895.

Leg Three: *such vile medicine to ingest*

Sword Swallower: poem is based on a photo by Diane Arbus, from her retrospective work, *Diane Arbus: An Aperture Monograph*, 25th Anniversary Edition, June 2005.

Katie Sandwina "Tosses Husband about like a Biscuit:" epigraph is taken from an anecdote about Enid Yandell in *Women Who Made a Difference* by Carol Crow-Carraco. Yandell (1870-1934) was a famed sculptor at the time she met Julia Grant, wife of Civil War General and United States President Ulysses S. Grant, while working on a project at the World Columbian Exposition in Chicago in 1893. Title for the poem is taken from promotional materials by the Barnum & Bailey Circus. Katie Sandwina (stage name, born Katie Brumbach, 1884-1952) feminized strongman Eugene Sandow's name after defeating him in a public weight-lifting competition. During her lifetime, Sandwina was the strongest person-male or female-on earth.

Popcorn Butcher: a 'butcher' is a circus word for 'vendor.'

Spidora Studies Spiderology: italicized portions of the text are taken from *The Noble Lyfe & Natures of Man, of Bestes, Serpentys, Fowels & Fisshes yt to be Most Knowen*, written in 1521 by Laurence Andrewes. It was an abridgment of the Dutch *Hortus Sanitatus* (1491), and contains one of the first illustrations of a spider in an orb-web. Only two copies of *The Noble Lyfe & Natures of Man* are known to exist.

Spidora Orders Curds and Whey: 'curds and whey' is an archaic term for 'cottage cheese.' The 'pie wagon' was the location where circus workers were fed; it was not open to the public. Patience Mouffet was the little girl immortalized in the nursery rhyme, "Little Miss Muffet." Her father, the Reverend Dr. Thomas Mouffet (1553-1604), was obsessed with spiders, and is known to have treated his daughter with spiders for illness.

Leg Four: *like joy corrodes the veins*

Spidora Dances the *Tarantella*: the *Tarantella* is a southern Italian folk dance that was said to cure victims of venomous spider bites.

Swarm: 'waggle dance' is a term for the figure-eight movement performed by honeybees to share directions to flower patch locations for gathering pollen.

Spidora Rides the *Spider*: the *Spider* is an amusement park ride, also known as the Octopus.

Spidora Sings to Spiders: 'Pepper's Ghost' is a technique for creating an illusion. By using glass and lighting, it can make objects seem to appear or disappear, or make one object seem to transform into something else.

Bird Millman Does *The Charleston*: Bird Millman (stage name; born Jennadean Engleman in 1890) became the most celebrated female high-wire performer of all time. Known for her agility and grace, she eschewed novelty stunts. She performed on

Broadway while the circus wintered.

Zazel Blasted Out of a Cannon: little is known of 'Zazel' (stage name, born Rosa Richter in 1862), other than the fact that she was the first cannonball stunt artist in 1877. Her act, known as the Eagle Swoop, was often imitated by other 'Zazels' hoping to capitalize on her fame.

'Tiny' Kline as Tinker Bell: 'Tiny' Kline (stage name; born Helen Deutsch in 1891) was one of the few women to successfully climb all the way up the circus career ladder, starting as a 'cooch girl,' then working as an acrobat and later a famous aerialist before retiring. Walt Disney hand-picked Kline as the first Tinker Bell to fly over Disneyland, asking her to come out of retirement. Kline was in her early 70s at the time.

Leg Five: *the gross unfortunate of dusk*

The Gilly Girls in Need: 'gilly' is circus slang for a member of the public, or someone from a local town; 'cherry pie' is circus slang for jobs taken on by circus folk for extra money during the season.

mother named Corbin seems very fond of it: poem inspired by a diary entry on May 31, 1869 from *The Heavens are Weeping: The Diaries of George R. Browder*, edited by Richard Trout. Italicized lines taken directly from Reverend Browder's entry.

Divine Woman: 'pickled punk' is circus slang for a dead fetus or newborn, often deformed, preserved in formaldehyde and placed on view in sideshows.

Spidora Shuns Arachnophobia: epigraph is taken from *The Book of the Spider: From Arachnophobia to the Love of Spiders* by Paul Hillyard.

Leg Six: *cropped locks and that curse*

Spidora Saves Spiders: epigraph haiku by Kobyashi Issa (1763-1827) translation by Robert Hass.

Sleight-of-Hand: poem is in response to the media coverage of the 2008 Democratic primaries.

Josie DeMott Robinson Attends a Rally: Josephine DeMott Robinson (1868-1948) was a famous bareback rider in the early 20th century and also a staunch suffragist. She would often attend rallies and pose for publicity photos. In 1912 she generated controversy by organizing the women in the Barnum & Bailey Circus to work for the suffrage movement, and also became captain of the suffrage club in her local home district.

Leg Seven: *fits of wakefulness when her lust is slaked*

Spidora Covets Silk Stockings: poem is based on an actual event; in 1709, Xavier Saint-Hilaire Bon of Montpellier presented the French Academy with gloves and stockings made from spider silk. This resulted in the completion of two studies in France in 1710 on the potential uses of spider silk to replace silkworms, and, while it was deemed expensive and impractical, the current Emperor of China requested translations of the study.

After Colette Performs *The Flesh* Outside Paris: Sidonie-Gabrielle Colette (1873-1954), most famous as a novelist, was also a music hall performer. In 1907 she toured in a pantomime, "*La Chair*," or "*The Flesh*," which was banned in several small provinces outside of Paris. This show is where the term "bodice-ripper," originated, as in one scene Colette's bodice is literally torn from her body in fury by another actor, leaving her near-naked onstage. In a letter dated September, 1908, Colette expresses her love of pantomime over any other kind of performing art.

A Treatise on Handling Snakes: poem draws liberally from the Pentecostal snake-handling ritual, including terms such as salvation: saving the soul from sin, the Holy Kiss form of greeting, and sanctification: to make holy or sacred. Pentecostal Christianity believes in the direct personal experience with God through the Holy Spirit. Snake handling comes from a literal interpretation of the Gospel of Mark, 16:18, which serves as the epigraph to the poem.

Spidora Receives a String of Pearls: epigraph is from the poem "The Study of a Spider" by John Leicester Warren, Lord de Tabley (1835-1895), who was a friend and contemporary of Tennyson.

Making Jenny Haniver: a 'Jenny Haniver' is a fake mermaid; creating such hoaxes has occurred since the 16th century, and while they have taken many forms, 'Jenny Haivers' most often refer to the fake mermaids made by slicing open a devilfish.

Lulu Lataska on the Cover: Lulu Lataska, (stage name; birth name and location unknown) was very involved in the public performance arena. She billed herself as an and actress, dancer, snake charmer, Circassian Woman, and necromancer/fortune teller. Her tag line was "Never to be Forgotten." The cover photo is from a promotional card taken in a photographer's studio in 1885.

Leg Eight: *each night behind closed blinds*

Spidora Defies Description: found poem taken from two texts; the first (italicized opening and last line) are lines taken from barker pitches for the spidora exhibit, the second text (regular lines; italics in original text) is taken from the *Insectorum Theatrum* (1634) by Reverend Dr. Thomas Mouffet, Patience Mouffet's father.

Greasepaint Graces: epigraph quotes opening each section taken from Louise Gluck's *Averno*. Part I is from section four of the poem "October," part II from the poem "A Myth of Innocence," and part III from the poem "Telescope," respectively. Part II's 23 found poem fragments (in italics) taken from a series of hand-scribbled notes and voice mail messages from summer 2007 to summer 2008; presented with slight changes to text. Both parties to remain anonymous.

Great-Aunt Josephine: First Lesson: 'Centauridies' is the name given to female Centaurs in Greek mythology.

'Marvelous May' Wirth Somersaults Forward: May Emmeline Wirth (1894-1978) became, along with 'Bird' Millman and Lillian Leitzel, one of the biggest stars in circus history. Known as the premiere bareback rider of the 20th century, Wirth was supposedly the only rider to ever execute a forward somersault on a galloping horse. She was never seen on circus grounds without her famous pink bow, which she wore until she retired in 1937.

Why Mata Hari Leaves the Circus: Mata Hari (stage name, born Margaretha Zelle, 1876-1917) was an exotic dancer in Paris during the fin de siècle. She was later executed by firing squad for espionage during World War I. Recently released documents from her trial imply that her status as a German spy was never fully proven. In 1904 Mata Hari spent a year with an equestrian circus in the rue Bénouville, before launching her exotic dancing career.

As Lillian Leitzel Reaches 249: Lillian Leitzel, (stage name, born Leopoldina Alitza Pelikan in Germany, 1882-1931), is known to this day as the 'Queen of the Arena.' Known for her demanding personality as well as her skill as an aerialist, Leitzel was also fluent in five languages and was an excellent pianist. Leitzel was known for her rotation of one-arm planges, where she would hurl her body over itself continuously. She commanded top billing longer than any other performer in circus history.

INDEX OF TITLES AND FIRST LINES

Poem titles are in bold, and the first lines are in regular text with page numbers on the right.

A **After Colette Performs *The Flesh* Outside of Paris**   85
Afterwards, she appraises   7
A modern House of Mirrors,   16
An Appetite for Glass   45
and still the woman   79
and the rooms will change   and the floors   72
and what would you do   61
Aprile and Mae   15
As Lillian Leitzel Reaches 249   106
At ninety mph she arcs over a parade of zebras   55
A Treatise on Handling Snakes   89
a winter without snow is like a drought   96
A woman slithers away   88
B Before she flits over Cinderella's castle   56
Bird Millman Does *The Charleston*   54
Burning Ballerina!   86
C Calliope breathes   xvi
carousel in winter   5
Clown Psalm   32
Contortionist   104
Crimson lipstick will go missing   52
D **Divine Woman**   63
Divorcing the Strong Man   105
Dogs come   63
Dusk.   66
E **Epilogue**   109
Eve Eating a Candy Apple   34
Evetta Matthews Clowns Around   33
F *fifteen sixteen*   37
find us through the fortune-teller: 58
first   74
Frenetic, her landlady cleans   73
from the high wire   75
G **Greasepaint Graces**   96
Great-Aunt Josephine: Anguine Hours   88
Great-Aunt Josephine: First Lesson   101
Great-Aunt Josephine: Loose Ends   52
Great-Aunt Josephine: Lost Photographs   9
Great-Aunt Josephine: Savory Gossip   42
Great-Aunt Josephine: Two-Way Mirror   16

H	Her apartment spills over with spider	64
	Her breath catches at the back	12
	Her mid-day meal consists of this dish.	46
	Hideous!	94
	Highwire Haiku	75
I	**inside the funhouse**	72
	In tights that show	33
	Invocation	xvi
	Isabelle Butler Rides *The Dip of Death*	10
	I sift through pictures, seeking your eyes,	9
	It rained for days,	82
	It's in the open air	59
	It's not the grey heft of elephants,	53
J	**Josie DeMott Robinson Attends a Rally**	82
	just another strange girl	34
K	**Katie Sandwina "Tosses Husband About Like a Biscuit"**	38
L	**Lament for Little Miss 1565**	30
	Like spider pheromones on thread,	48
	Little Accuracy	67
	Lucia Zora Atop Snyder the Elephant	6
	Lulu Lataska on the Cover	92
M	**Mabel Stark Misses Her Tigers**	20
	Making Jenny Haniver	91
	'Marvelous May' Wirth Somersaults Forward	102
	May leaps with her feet in baskets	102
	Mermaid	2
	Mirth & Mayhem	18
	mother named Corbin seems very fond of it	61
	Mrs. Sibilant's Splendid Hair Tonic	65
	Muscles bulge from her bare arms	38
O	Once, she craved the solitude	41
	One pulse of a circus: the hum of cotton candy	18
	Only the air is dizzy, not Leitzel,	106
	On the third day after her mauling,	20
	organ grinder	51
P	**Popcorn Butcher**	39
	Portrait of a Young Woman as Poet	7
S	She	49
	She agrees to receive the police	85
	She could measure them	90
	She craves the sultry	39
	She dances brisk kick steps	54
	She enters the wooden	103
	She fixates on palm trees: the way the leaves crown the trunk	70
	She insists on assisting in the creation	8
	She is patient, although indecisive,	87
	She loves the imperfect legs:	4
	She obsesses over the caress	84

She refuses to speak of dreams that haunted her   103
She reminisces about her lovers   107
She strips to painted skin,   11
she tries so hard   *21*
She turns pages in books so old   43
sleight-of-hand   79
Some nights she slumbers with serpents, cold and coiled   89
s p i d e r   web   s p i d e r   14
Spidora Contemplates Children   64
Spidora Covets Silk Stockings   84
Spidora Craves Attention   68
Spidora Dances the *Tarantella*   48
Spidora Defies Description   94
Spidora Embraces Widowhood   107
Spidora Embroiders Her Words   14
Spidora Finds Religion   21
Spidora Identifies with Flies   41
Spidora Orders Curds and Whey   46
Spidora Polishes her Toes   12
Spidora Pulls the Legs Off Spiders   59
Spidora Purchases Pumps   87
Spidora Receives a String of Pearls   90
Spidora Rides the *Spider*   50
Spidora Saves Spiders   73
Spidora Shuns Arachnophobia   66
Spidora Sings to Spiders   53
Spidora Studies Spiderology   43
Spidora Undergoes *Metamorphosis*   *8*
Spidora Views Cave Art   4
Spidora Visits Mississippi   70
Swarm   49
Sword Swallower   36
T   televisions loom   in corners   68
Thalia, the Alley is no place to pray--   32
the blind bear   51
The car is waiting.   10
The Fat Lady Hums to Herself in Autumn   37
The fin leaves her thighs   2
The Gilly Girls in Need   58
The knife thrower trains her daughter   67
The lady with a beard   80
the never retrieved   105
The room holds fantasia, with *Payasos*   13
These Jennys will give head to the Devil   91
The skirt above her calves teased flames   86
The Tattooed Woman   11
The tawdry carnival tent's dark canvas   36
the woman on the platform clutches   109

They speak openly in the kitchen, amid bubbling 42
this carved whimsy 5
This mistress of the serpentine 92
Those lasses pose their hair at each sideshow: 65
'Tiny' Kline as Tinker Bell 56
To end, 45
Two Bearded Ladies 80
two circus cherubs 15
W **When a Circus Troupe Kidnapped María Izquierdo** 13
When she slips inside the cart 50
When the ponderous pachyderm rises 6
Why Mata Hari Leaves the Circus 103
why the two-headed juggler is female 74
Y You can see the mare's breath 101
Your white dress shows smudges of mud 30
Z **Zazel Blasted Out of a Cannon** 55

About the Poet

Joanie DiMartino has work published in many literary journals and anthologies. Her first chapbook, *Licking the Spoon*, was published in 2007. She is a past winner of the Betty Gabehart Award for poetry from the Women Writers Conference, Kentucky, and was a finalist in the Cultural Center of Cape Cod poetry competition.

Her poems have been featured in several art exhibits in Lexington, Kentucky, including *Sideshow*, a collaborative project with the Women Artists Group; *Collaborations + Catalysts*, an exhibit highlighting combined mediums; and *Connections--We Are All One*, an interfaith exhibit, where her poem, "The Monks," an experimental piece incorporating Gregorian Chant throughout the poem, was performed. DiMartino has had several poems presented by the East Haddam Plays & Players as part of their *Plays & Poetry* performance in selected locations throughout Connecticut. She was most recently featured in the exhibit *Women in the Arts*, a show by local artist Deborah Curtis, where her portrait and poem, "Self-Portrait," were on display at ArtWorks in Norwich, Connecticut.

She is currently at work on several projects, including a collection of poems about the 19th-century whaling industry, a collection of persona poems from the perspective of militant suffragist Alice Paul, a haiku sequence/female nude collaboration with visual artist Deborah Curtis, a haibun children's book with musician and illustrator Don Sineti, and the editing of two anthologies. Fabric artist Alison Luff is interpreting a selection of DiMartino's poems in textiles, and her work is being translated into several languages.

DiMartino holds an MA in public history from Rutgers University. She worked in the history museum field for over fifteen years, and her poetry often pairs history with a feminist perspective. She is a founding member of the women's poetry group Mosaic, in Lexington, Kentucky, and is currently also a member of Poets & Writers Consortium East in Groton, CT. She hosts Soup & Sonnets, a monthly literary salon for women, and, along with performing poetry, she reviews books and leads workshops and discussion groups. Raised in southern New Jersey, DiMartino has lived in Lexington, Kentucky, and now resides with her son in Mystic, CT.